D0410215

A PARRAGON BOOK

Published by Parragon Book Service Ltd,
Units 13-17, Avonbridge Trading Estate, Atlantic Road,
Avonmouth, Bristol BS11 9QD

Produced by The Templar Company plc,
Pippbrook Mill, London Road, Dorking,
Surrey RH4 1JE

Copyright © 1996 Parragon Book Service Limited

Edited by Robert Snedden
Designed by Mark Summersby

All rights reserved.

Printed and bound in the UK

ISBN 0 7525 1677 9

Photographic Acknowledgements:
Bruce Coleman Ltd: David R. Austen 15, Adrian Davies 16, Henneghien 18,
Luiz Claudio Marigo 21, Michael Klinec 24, Brian Henderson 26, Guido Cozzi
30, Kim Taylor 32, Michael Klinec 35, Norman Tomalin 37, Neil McAllister 38,
Fred Bruemmer 43, Steven C. Kaufman 45, Frans Lanting 46, Christer
Fredriksson 51, Brian Henderson 57, Clive Hicks 62, Brian Henderson 66, Erik
Bjurstrom 69, Neil McAllister 71, Andy Price 73, Clive Hicks 74, Luiz Claudio
Marigo 76, Christian Zuber 79, George McCarthy 80, Geoff Dore 82, Guido
Cozzi 84, Robert Wanscheidt 87.

FLPA: Panda/ L. Bucci 23, Silvestris 29, E & D Hosking 41, Panda/ L. Bucci
49, Derek Hall 53, Ian Cartwright 54, P. Mullen 59, P. Ward 60, D. Haigh 64.

Robert Harding Picture Library: Chris Rennie 13.

FACTFINDERS

FLAGS
· OF THE ·
WORLD

‖ ·PARRAGON· ‖

CONTENTS

INTRODUCTION

The first flags were probably invented either in India or in China. A Chinese ruler who lived more than three thousand years ago is said to have had a white banner carried before him. Chinese flags bore tigers, birds or dragons and were carried on chariots and planted on the walls of captured cities. The royal flag was special and it was a crime even to touch the flagbearer.

From India and China the use of flags spread to South-east Asia. The Saracens probably brought them to Europe. Islamic flags were greatly simplified and were probably plain black, white or red. In Europe, the first national flags appeared in the Middle Ages with many leaders adopting the flag of their particular patron saint so that in England the cross of St George was adopted and in Scotland the cross of St Andrew became the national flag. The oldest European flags are those that show the Christian cross.

The colours of national flags usually reflect the history, religion or culture of the particular country they represent. In the twelfth and thirteenth centuries European royalty had coats of arms that were incorporated into their flags. These can still be seen in the flags of Austria, San Marino and Liechtenstein.

Following the French Revolution in 1789 France adopted a red, white and blue flag. These colours had been associated with revolution and the struggle for freedom because they were also the colours that appeared in the flag of the Netherlands, a country involved in a long and bitter war for independence from Spain. Other countries in Europe and Central and South America adopted three-coloured flags of their own to represent their own belief in the three principles of the French Revolution – liberty, equality and fraternity.

The choice of colours for the flags of the Middle East has, in most cases, been limited to the traditional colours of Islam – red, white, green and black. Most Arab states use a combination of these colours in a tricolour flag. Some Muslim countries, such as Pakistan, Turkey and Malaysia, also feature the crescent moon and star, which has become the accepted symbol of Islam since it was adopted by the Turks in the thirteenth century. Several Asian countries feature religious symbols on their flags, for example a wheel on the Indian flag, a yin-yang symbol on the flags of Mongolia and South Korea and the Sun in the flags of Japan and Taiwan.

Today flags may be used occasionally for display and decoration, but they still retain their power to act as a rallying point, as a symbolic manifestation of the country they represent and of the beliefs and aspirations of its peoples.

AFGHANISTAN

AREA	647,500 sq km
POPULATION	24,227,000
CAPITAL	Kabul
LANGUAGE	Pushtu, Dari
RELIGION	Sunni Muslim, Shi'a Muslim
CURRENCY	Afghani

ALBANIA

AREA	28,748 sq km
POPULATION	3,471,000
CAPITAL	Tirana
LANGUAGE	Albanian
RELIGION	Muslim, Orthodox
CURRENCY	Lek

ALGERIA

AREA	2,381,741 sq km
POPULATION	29,180,000
CAPITAL	Algiers
LANGUAGE	Arabic, French
RELIGION	Muslim
CURRENCY	Algerian dinar

ANDORRA

AREA	450 sq km
POPULATION	68,000
CAPITAL	Andorra la Vella
LANGUAGE	Catalan
RELIGION	Roman Catholic
CURRENCY	Franc & Peseta

The twelfth-century church of Sant Marti nestles in the tiny mountain country of Andorra.

ANGOLA

AREA	1,246,700 sq km
POPULATION	10,339,000
CAPITAL	Luanda
LANGUAGE	Portuguese, Bantu
RELIGION	Indigenous beliefs
CURRENCY	Kwanza

ANTIGUA & BARBUDA

AREA	442 sq km
POPULATION	65,000
CAPITAL	St John's
LANGUAGE	English,
RELIGION	Protestant
CURRENCY	E. Caribbean dollar

ARGENTINA

AREA	2,766,890 sq km
POPULATION	34,300,000
CAPITAL	Buenos Aires
LANGUAGE	Spanish
RELIGION	Roman Catholic
CURRENCY	Peso

ARMENIA

AREA	29,800 sq km
POPULATION	3,600,000
CAPITAL	Yerevan
LANGUAGE	Armenian
RELIGION	Orthodox
CURRENCY	Ruble

AUSTRALIA

AREA	7,686,850 sq km
POPULATION	18,500,000
CAPITAL	Canberra
LANGUAGE	English
RELIGION	Anglican, Roman Catholic
CURRENCY	Australian dollar

The Sydney Opera House is one of Australia's most famous landmarks.

AUSTRIA

AREA	83,857 sq km
POPULATION	8,000,000
CAPITAL	Vienna
LANGUAGE	German
RELIGION	Roman Catholic
CURRENCY	Austrian schilling

AZERBAIJAN

AREA	86,600 sq km
POPULATION	7,800,000
CAPITAL	Baku
LANGUAGE	Azeri, Russian
RELIGION	Muslim, Orthodox
CURRENCY	Manat

THE BAHAMAS

AREA	13,940 sq km
POPULATION	277,000
CAPITAL	Nassau
LANGUAGE	English
RELIGION	Baptist, Roman Catholic
CURRENCY	Bahamian dollar

The Parliament Building in Nassau, capital of the Bahamas.

16

BAHRAIN

AREA	620 sq km
POPULATION	605,000
CAPITAL	Manama
LANGUAGE	Arabic
RELIGION	Islam
CURRENCY	Bahraini dinar

BANGLADESH

AREA	143,998 sq km
POPULATION	128,000,000
CAPITAL	Dhaka
LANGUAGE	Bangla, English
RELIGION	Muslim, Hindu
CURRENCY	Taka

BARBADOS

AREA	430 sq km
POPULATION	260,000
CAPITAL	Bridgetown
LANGUAGE	English
RELIGION	Protestant
CURRENCY	Barbadian dollar

BELARUS

AREA	207,600
POPULATION	10,500,000
CAPITAL	Minsk
LANGUAGE	Byelorussian
RELIGION	Orthodox
CURRENCY	Ruble

BELGIUM

AREA	30,518 sq km
POPULATION	10,100,000
CAPITAL	Brussels
LANGUAGE	Flemish, French
RELIGION	Roman Catholic, Protestant
CURRENCY	Belgian franc

The ancient town of Bruges in Belgium has many fine buildings. Once an important trading centre, it is famous for its lace.

BELIZE

AREA	22,963 sq km
POPULATION	215,000
CAPITAL	Belmopan
LANGUAGE	English, Spanish
RELIGION	Roman Catholic, Protestant
CURRENCY	Belizean dollar

BENIN

AREA	112,622 sq km
POPULATION	5,530,000
CAPITAL	Porto-Novo
LANGUAGE	French, Tribal
RELIGION	Indigenous beliefs
CURRENCY	CFA franc

BHUTAN

AREA	47,000 sq km
POPULATION	1,400,000
CAPITAL	Thimphu
LANGUAGE	Dzongkha
RELIGION	Buddhist, Hindu
CURRENCY	Ngultrum

BOLIVIA

AREA	1,098,581 sq km
POPULATION	7,950,000
CAPITAL	La Paz
LANGUAGE	Spanish
RELIGION	Roman Catholic
CURRENCY	Boliviano

BOSNIA & HERZEGOVINA

AREA	51,129
POPULATION	3,200,000
CAPITAL	Sarajevo
LANGUAGE	Serbo-Croat
RELIGION	Muslim, Orthodox, Catholic
CURRENCY	Dinar

BOTSWANA

AREA	600,370 sq km
POPULATION	1,400,000
CAPITAL	Gaborone
LANGUAGE	English, Setswana
RELIGION	Tribal, Christian
CURRENCY	Pula

BRAZIL

AREA	8,511,996 sq km
POPULATION	161,000,000
CAPITAL	Brasília
LANGUAGE	Portuguese
RELIGION	Roman Catholic
CURRENCY	Cruzeiro real

Sugar Loaf Mountain dominates the view across Guanabara Bay, Rio de Janeiro, Brazil.

BRUNEI

AREA	5,765 sq km
POPULATION	295,000
CAPITAL	Bandar Seri Begawan
LANGUAGE	Malay
RELIGION	Muslim, Buddhist
CURRENCY	Bruneian dollar

BULGARIA

AREA	110,912 sq km
POPULATION	8,700,000
CAPITAL	Sofia
LANGUAGE	Bulgarian
RELIGION	Orthodox, Muslim
CURRENCY	Lev

BURKINA FASO

AREA	274,122 sq km
POPULATION	10,714,000
CAPITAL	Ouagadougou
LANGUAGE	French, Tribal
RELIGION	Muslim, indigenous beliefs
CURRENCY	CFA franc

BURMA

AREA	678,500 sq km
POPULATION	45,900,000
CAPITAL	Rangoon
LANGUAGE	Burmese
RELIGION	Buddhist
CURRENCY	Kyat

BURUNDI

AREA	27,834 sq km
POPULATION	6,400,000
CAPITAL	Bujumbura
LANGUAGE	Kirundi, French
RELIGION	Roman Catholic, indigenous beliefs
CURRENCY	Burundi franc

CAMBODIA

AREA	181,035 sq km
POPULATION	10,860,000
CAPITAL	Phnom Penh
LANGUAGE	Khmer
RELIGION	Buddhist
CURRENCY	Riel

A Buddhist monk in traditional saffron robes outside the temple of Angkor Vat, Cambodia.

CAMEROON

AREA	475,442 sq km
POPULATION	13,915,000
CAPITAL	Yaoundé
LANGUAGE	French, English, African languages
RELIGION	Indigenous beliefs, Christian
CURRENCY	CFA franc

CANADA

AREA	9,976,610 sq km
POPULATION	28,745,000
CAPITAL	Ottawa
LANGUAGE	English, French
RELIGION	Roman Catholic, Protestant
CURRENCY	Canadian dollar

The CN Tower dominates the Toronto skyline. Toronto, on Lake Ontario, is Canada's second largest city.

CAPE VERDE

AREA	4,033 sq km
POPULATION	449,000
CAPITAL	Praia
LANGUAGE	Portuguese, Crioulo
RELIGION	Roman Catholic
CURRENCY	Cape Verde escudo

CENTRAL AFRICAN REPUBLIC

AREA	622,980 sq km
POPULATION	2,900,000
CAPITAL	Bangui
LANGUAGE	French, Sangho
RELIGION	Animist, Christian, Muslim
CURRENCY	CFA franc

CHAD

AREA	1,284,000 sq km
POPULATION	5,707,000
CAPITAL	N'djaména
LANGUAGE	French, Arabic
RELIGION	Muslim, Christian
CURRENCY	CFA franc

CHILE

AREA	756,945 sq km
POPULATION	14,372,000
CAPITAL	Santiago
LANGUAGE	Spanish
RELIGION	Roman Catholic
CURRENCY	Chilean peso

CHINA

AREA	9,596,900 sq km
POPULATION	1,215,000,000
CAPITAL	Beijing
LANGUAGE	Mandarin Chinese, other dialects
RELIGION	Daoist, Buddhist
CURRENCY	Yuan

The Great Wall of China was largely built in the 15th and 16th centuries. It is nearly 2400km (1500 miles) long and around 9 metres (30 feet) high.

COLOMBIA

AREA	1,138,910 sq km
POPULATION	36,815,000
CAPITAL	Bogatá
LANGUAGE	Spanish
RELIGION	Roman Catholic
CURRENCY	Colombian peso

COMOROS

AREA	2170 sq km
POPULATION	568,000
CAPITAL	Moroni
LANGUAGE	Arabic, French
RELIGION	Sunni Muslim
CURRENCY	Comoran franc

CONGO

AREA	342,000 sq km
POPULATION	2,560,000
CAPITAL	Brazzaville
LANGUAGE	French, Lingala, Kikongo
RELIGION	Christian, Animist
CURRENCY	CFA franc

COSTA RICA

AREA	51,100 sq km
POPULATION	3,495,000
CAPITAL	San José
LANGUAGE	Spanish
RELIGION	Roman Catholic
CURRENCY	Costa Rican colón

CROATIA

AREA	56,538 sq km
POPULATION	4,670,000
CAPITAL	Zagreb
LANGUAGE	Serbo-Croat
RELIGION	Roman Catholic, Orthodox
CURRENCY	Dinar

CUBA

AREA	110,860 sq km
POPULATION	11,000,000
CAPITAL	Havana
LANGUAGE	Spanish
RELIGION	Roman Catholic
CURRENCY	Cuban peso

CYPRUS

AREA	9,251 sq km
POPULATION	742,000
CAPITAL	Nicosia
LANGUAGE	Greek, Turkish, English
RELIGION	Greek Orthodox, Muslim
CURRENCY	Cyprus pound

CZECH REPUBLIC

AREA	78,703 sq km
POPULATION	10,460,000
CAPITAL	Prague
LANGUAGE	Czech, Slovak
RELIGION	Atheist, Roman Catholic, Protestant
CURRENCY	Koruna

Prague, the capital of the Czech Republic, is an important centre of industry and culture on the banks of the River Vltava.

DENMARK

AREA	43,075 sq km
POPULATION	5,210,000
CAPITAL	Copenhagen
LANGUAGE	Danish, Faroese
RELIGION	Lutheran
CURRENCY	Danish Krone

Holckenhavn Castle on the Danish island of Fyn.

DJIBOUTI

AREA	22,000 sq km
POPULATION	427,000
CAPITAL	Djibouti
LANGUAGE	French, Arabic
RELIGION	Muslim
CURRENCY	Djibouti franc

DOMINICA

AREA	751 sq km
POPULATION	83,000
CAPITAL	Roseau
LANGUAGE	English, French patois
RELIGION	Roman Catholic, Protestant
CURRENCY	E. Caribbean dollar

DOMINICAN REPUBLIC

AREA	48,730 sq km
POPULATION	7,600,000
CAPITAL	Santo Domingo
LANGUAGE	Spanish
RELIGION	Roman Catholic
CURRENCY	Dominica peso

ECUADOR

AREA	283,561 sq km
POPULATION	11,100,000
CAPITAL	Quito
LANGUAGE	Spanish, Quechua
RELIGION	Roman Catholic
CURRENCY	Sucre

EGYPT

AREA	1,450,000 sq km
POPULATION	63,580,000
CAPITAL	Cairo
LANGUAGE	Arabic
RELIGION	Sunni Muslim
CURRENCY	Egyptian pound

The Great Pyramids of Giza, built between 2600 and 2500BC, to house the remains of some of Ancient Egypt's rulers.

EL SALVADOR

AREA	21,040 sq km
POPULATION	5,990,000
CAPITAL	San Salvador
LANGUAGE	Spanish
RELIGION	Roman Catholic
CURRENCY	Colón

EQUATORIAL GUINEA

AREA	28,050 sq km
POPULATION	417,000
CAPITAL	Malabo
LANGUAGE	Spanish, Pidgin English
RELIGION	Roman Catholic
CURRENCY	CFA franc

ERITREA

AREA	121,320 sq km
POPULATION	3,900,000
CAPITAL	Asmara
LANGUAGE	Tigre, Kunama
RELIGION	Christian, Muslim
CURRENCY	Ethiopian birr

ESTONIA

AREA	45,100
POPULATION	1,634,000
CAPITAL	Tallin
LANGUAGE	Estonian, Russian
RELIGION	Lutheran
CURRENCY	Ruble

ETHIOPIA

AREA	1,127,127 sq km
POPULATION	57,700,000
CAPITAL	Addis Ababa
LANGUAGE	Amharic, Tigrinya, others
RELIGION	Muslim, Orthodox
CURRENCY	Ethiopian birr

FIJI

AREA	18,270 sq km
POPULATION	782,000
CAPITAL	Suva
LANGUAGE	English, Fijian, Hindustani
RELIGION	Christian, Hindu
CURRENCY	Fijian dollar

FINLAND

AREA	337,030 sq km
POPULATION	5,100,000
CAPITAL	Helsinki
LANGUAGE	Finnish
RELIGION	Lutheran
CURRENCY	Markka

FRANCE

AREA	547,030 sq km
POPULATION	58,375,000
CAPITAL	Paris
LANGUAGE	French
RELIGION	Roman Catholic
CURRENCY	French franc

The Eiffel Tower, built in 1889 and standing 300 metres (984 feet) high, is one of the most famous sights of Paris, France.

GABON

AREA	267,670 sq km
POPULATION	1,173,000
CAPITAL	Libreville
LANGUAGE	French, Fang, others
RELIGION	Christian, Animist
CURRENCY	CFA franc

THE GAMBIA

AREA	11,300 sq km
POPULATION	1,020,000
CAPITAL	Banjul
LANGUAGE	English, Mandinka, Wolof
RELIGION	Muslim
CURRENCY	Gambian dalasi

GEORGIA

AREA	69,700 sq km
POPULATION	5,770,000
CAPITAL	Tbilisi
LANGUAGE	Georgian, Russian
RELIGION	Orthodox
CURRENCY	Ruble

GERMANY

AREA	356,910 sq km
POPULATION	81,550,000
CAPITAL	Berlin
LANGUAGE	German
RELIGION	Protestant, Roman Catholic
CURRENCY	Deutsche mark

GHANA

AREA	238,540 sq km
POPULATION	18,300,000
CAPITAL	Accra
LANGUAGE	English, African languages
RELIGION	Christian, Muslim, indigenous beliefs
CURRENCY	Cedi

GREECE

AREA	131,940 sq km
POPULATION	10,720,000
CAPITAL	Athens
LANGUAGE	Greek
RELIGION	Greek Orthodox
CURRENCY	Drachma

The Parthenon, Athens, is one of the glories of Ancient Greek architecture. It was built between 447 and 432BC.

GRENADA

AREA 340 sq km
POPULATION 94,500
CAPITAL St George's
LANGUAGE English, French
RELIGION Roman Catholic
CURRENCY E. Caribbean dollar

GUATEMALA

AREA 108,890 sq km
POPULATION 11,276,000
CAPITAL Guatemala City
LANGUAGE Spanish
RELIGION Roman Catholic
CURRENCY Quetzal

The impressive cathedral in Guatemala City was built in 1815. It survived a series of earthquakes that shook the city for six weeks in 1917–18.

GUINEA

AREA	245,860 sq km
POPULATION	6,700,000
CAPITAL	Conakry
LANGUAGE	French
RELIGION	Muslim
CURRENCY	Guinea franc

GUINEA-BISSAU

AREA	36,125 sq km
POPULATION	1,150,000
CAPITAL	Bissau
LANGUAGE	Portuguese, Criolo
RELIGION	Indigenous beliefs, Muslim
CURRENCY	Peso Guineano

GUYANA

AREA	214,970 sq km
POPULATION	718,000
CAPITAL	Georgetown
LANGUAGE	English, dialects
RELIGION	Christian, Hindu
CURRENCY	Guyana dollar

HAITI

AREA	27,750 sq km
POPULATION	6,549,000
CAPITAL	Port-au-Prince
LANGUAGE	French, Creole
RELIGION	Roman Catholic, Voodoo
CURRENCY	Gourde

HONDURAS

AREA	112,090 sq km
POPULATION	5,600,000
CAPITAL	Tegucigalpa
LANGUAGE	Spanish
RELIGION	Roman Catholic
CURRENCY	Lempira

HUNGARY

AREA	93,030 sq km
POPULATION	10,320,000
CAPITAL	Budapest
LANGUAGE	Hungarian
RELIGION	Roman Catholic, Protestant
CURRENCY	Forint

ICELAND

AREA	103,000 sq km
POPULATION	268,000
CAPITAL	Reykjavík
LANGUAGE	Icelandic
RELIGION	Lutheran
CURRENCY	Krona

The Main Square in Reykjavík, capital city of Iceland. Most people live around the coast of this country of glaciers and volcanoes.

INDIA

AREA	3,278,590 sq km
POPULATION	953,123,000
CAPITAL	Delhi
LANGUAGE	English, over 20 other languages
RELIGION	Hindu, Muslim
CURRENCY	Rupee

INDONESIA

AREA 1,919,443 sq km
POPULATION 206,760,000
CAPITAL Jakarta
LANGUAGE Bahasa Indonesia
RELIGION Muslim
CURRENCY Rupiah

IRAN

AREA 1,648,000 sq km
POPULATION 66,105,000
CAPITAL Tehran
LANGUAGE Persian dialects
RELIGION Shi'a Muslim
CURRENCY Iranian riyal

IRAQ

AREA 437,072 sq km
POPULATION 21,412,000
CAPITAL Baghdad
LANGUAGE Arabic, Kurdish
RELIGION Shi'a Muslim, Sunni Muslim
CURRENCY Iraqi dinar

IRELAND

AREA	70,283 sq km
POPULATION	3,560,000
CAPITAL	Dublin
LANGUAGE	English, Gaelic
RELIGION	Roman Catholic
CURRENCY	Punt

ISRAEL

AREA	20,770 sq km
POPULATION	5,510,000
CAPITAL	Jerusalem
LANGUAGE	Hebrew, Arabic
RELIGION	Judaism, Sunni Muslim
CURRENCY	New Israel shekel

The Negev Desert covers around 12,000 sq km (4632 sq miles) of southern Israel. Irrigation has allowed some farming to be established here.

ITALY

AREA	301,230 sq km
POPULATION	58,384,000
CAPITAL	Rome
LANGUAGE	Italian
RELIGION	Roman Catholic
CURRENCY	Italian lira

IVORY COAST

AREA	322,463 sq km
POPULATION	15,290,000
CAPITAL	Abidjan
LANGUAGE	French, dialects
RELIGION	Indigenous beliefs, Muslim
CURRENCY	CFA franc

JAMAICA

AREA	10,990 sq km
POPULATION	2,594,000
CAPITAL	Kingston
LANGUAGE	English, Creole
RELIGION	Protestant, spiritual cults
CURRENCY	Jamaican dollar

JAPAN

AREA	377,835 sq km
POPULATION	125,910,000
CAPITAL	Tokyo
LANGUAGE	Japanese
RELIGION	Buddhist, Shintoist
CURRENCY	Japanese yen

The Daibutsuden in Nara, Japan, is the world's largest wooden building. Nara was the first capital city of Japan.

JORDAN

AREA	89,213 sq km
POPULATION	4,110,000
CAPITAL	Amman
LANGUAGE	Arabic
RELIGION	Sunni Muslim
CURRENCY	Jordan dinar

KAZAKHSTAN

AREA	2,717,300 sq km
POPULATION	17,485,000
CAPITAL	Alma-Ata
LANGUAGE	Russian, Kazakh
RELIGION	Orthodox, Muslim
CURRENCY	Ruble

KENYA

AREA	582,650 sq km
POPULATION	29,100,000
CAPITAL	Nairobi
LANGUAGE	Swahili, English
RELIGION	Christian, indigenous beliefs
CURRENCY	Kenyan shilling

A herd of giraffe in the Masai Mara National Park, Kenya, one of many wildlife reserves in the country.

KIRIBATI

AREA	717 sq km
POPULATION	80,000
CAPITAL	Tarawa
LANGUAGE	Gilbertese, English
RELIGION	Protestant, Roman Catholic
CURRENCY	Australian dollar

KOREA, NORTH

AREA	120,540 sq km
POPULATION	23,900,000
CAPITAL	Pyongyang
LANGUAGE	Korean
RELIGION	Buddhist, Confucist
CURRENCY	Won

KOREA, SOUTH

AREA	98,480 sq km
POPULATION	46,000,000
CAPITAL	Seoul
LANGUAGE	Korean
RELIGION	Buddhist, Confucist
CURRENCY	Won

KUWAIT

AREA	17,820 sq km
POPULATION	1,952,000
CAPITAL	Kuwait
LANGUAGE	Arabic
RELIGION	Shi'a Muslim, Sunni Muslim
CURRENCY	Kuwaiti dinar

KYRGYZSTAN

AREA	198,500 sq km
POPULATION	4,840,000
CAPITAL	Frunze
LANGUAGE	Kyrgyz, Russian
RELIGION	Orthodox, Muslim
CURRENCY	Ruble

LAOS

AREA	236,800 sq km
POPULATION	4,974,000
CAPITAL	Vientiane
LANGUAGE	Lao
RELIGION	Buddhist, Animist
CURRENCY	Kip

Laos is predominantly a Buddhist country. This figure of Buddha sits under the 'Tree of Illumination' in Vientiane, the capital city.

LATVIA

AREA	64,100 sq km
POPULATION	2,777,000
CAPITAL	Riga
LANGUAGE	Lettish, Russian
RELIGION	Orthodox, Lutheran, Roman Catholic
CURRENCY	Ruble

LEBANON

AREA	10,400 sq km
POPULATION	3,700,000
CAPITAL	Beirut
LANGUAGE	Arabic, French
RELIGION	Muslim, Christian
CURRENCY	Lebanese pound

LESOTHO

AREA	30,350 sq km
POPULATION	2,040,000
CAPITAL	Maseru
LANGUAGE	Sesotho, English
RELIGION	Christian, indigenous beliefs
CURRENCY	Loti

LIBERIA

AREA	111,370 sq km
POPULATION	3,175,000
CAPITAL	Monrovia
LANGUAGE	English, Tribal
RELIGION	Muslim, Tribal
CURRENCY	Liberian dollar

LIBYA

AREA	1,759,540 sq km
POPULATION	5,440,000
CAPITAL	Tripoli
LANGUAGE	Arabic
RELIGION	Sunni Muslim
CURRENCY	Lybian dinar

LIECHTENSTEIN

AREA	160 sq km
POPULATION	31,000
CAPITAL	Vaduz
LANGUAGE	German, Alemannic
RELIGION	Roman Catholic
CURRENCY	Swiss franc

The Royal Castle of Vaduz, capital of the tiny country of Liechtenstein, is the home of the ruling prince.

LITHUANIA

AREA	65,200 sq km
POPULATION	3,900,000
CAPITAL	Vilnius
LANGUAGE	Lithuanian, Russian
RELIGION	Lutheran, Roman Catholic
CURRENCY	Ruble

LUXEMBOURG

AREA	2,586 sq km
POPULATION	407,000
CAPITAL	Luxembourg
LANGUAGE	French, German, Luxembourgisch
RELIGION	Roman Catholic
CURRENCY	Luxembourg franc

MACEDONIA

AREA	25,333 sq km
POPULATION	2,180,000
CAPITAL	Skopje
LANGUAGE	Macedonian, Albanian
RELIGION	Orthodox, Muslim
CURRENCY	Macedonian dinar

MADAGASCAR

AREA	587,040 sq km
POPULATION	14,300,000
CAPITAL	Antananarivo
LANGUAGE	Malagasy, French
RELIGION	Animist, Christian
CURRENCY	Malagasy franc

MALAWI

AREA	118,480 sq km
POPULATION	10,065,000
CAPITAL	Lilongwe
LANGUAGE	English, Chichewa
RELIGION	Christian, Muslim
CURRENCY	Kwacha

MALAYSIA

AREA	329,750 sq km
POPULATION	20,165,000
CAPITAL	Kuala Lumpur
LANGUAGE	Malay, English
RELIGION	Muslim, Christian, Buddhist
CURRENCY	Ringgit

Terraces have been carved out of this wooded hillside on Panang Island, Malaysia, to provide growing space for vegetable crops.

MALDIVES

AREA	300 sq km
POPULATION	270,000
CAPITAL	Malé
LANGUAGE	Divehi
RELIGION	Sunni Muslim
CURRENCY	Rufiyaa

An idyllic beach scene on Nakatchafushi Island, one of the Maldives, which consist of a large number of small coral islands.

MALI

AREA	1,240,192 sq km
POPULATION	9,646,000
CAPITAL	Bamako
LANGUAGE	French, Bambara
RELIGION	Muslim
CURRENCY	Mali franc

MALTA

AREA	320 sq km
POPULATION	373,000
CAPITAL	Valletta
LANGUAGE	English, Maltese
RELIGION	Roman Catholic
CURRENCY	Maltese lira

MAURITANIA

AREA	1,030,700 sq km
POPULATION	2,335,000
CAPITAL	Nouakchott
LANGUAGE	Arabic, Wolof
RELIGION	Muslim
CURRENCY	Mauritanian ouguiya

MAURITIUS

AREA	1860 sq km
POPULATION	1,137,000
CAPITAL	Port Louis
LANGUAGE	English, Creole, others
RELIGION	Hindu, Christian
CURRENCY	Mauritian rupee

MEXICO

AREA	1,972,550 sq km
POPULATION	95,772,000
CAPITAL	Mexico City
LANGUAGE	Spanish
RELIGION	Roman Catholic
CURRENCY	Mexican peso

MOLDOVA

AREA	33,700 sq km
POPULATION	4,506,000
CAPITAL	Kishinev
LANGUAGE	Moldovan, Russian
RELIGION	Orthodox
CURRENCY	Ruble

MONACO

AREA	1.95 sq km
POPULATION	31,700
CAPITAL	Monaco
LANGUAGE	French
RELIGION	Roman Catholic
CURRENCY	French franc

MONGOLIA

AREA	1,565,000 sq km
POPULATION	2,558,000
CAPITAL	Ulan Bator
LANGUAGE	Khalka Mongol
RELIGION	Buddhist
CURRENCY	Tugrik

A yurt, the traditional dwelling of the nomadic Mongolians. This one is part of a suburb of the capital, Ulan Bator.

MOROCCO

AREA	446,550 sq km
POPULATION	29,777,000
CAPITAL	Rabat
LANGUAGE	Arabic, Berber dialects
RELIGION	Muslim
CURRENCY	Moroccan dirham

MOZAMBIQUE

AREA	801,590 sq km
POPULATION	18,635,000
CAPITAL	Maputo
LANGUAGE	Portuguese, dialects
RELIGION	Indigenous beliefs, Muslim
CURRENCY	Metical

NAMIBIA

AREA	825,418 sq km
POPULATION	1,710,000
CAPITAL	Windhoek
LANGUAGE	English, Afrikaans, German
RELIGION	Christian
CURRENCY	South African rand

NAURU

AREA	21 sq km
POPULATION	10,200
CAPITAL	Yaren
LANGUAGE	Nauruan, English
RELIGION	Protestant, Roman Catholic
CURRENCY	Australian dollar

NEPAL

AREA	148,800 sq km
POPULATION	22,100,000
CAPITAL	Kathmandu
LANGUAGE	Nepali, dialects
RELIGION	Hindu
CURRENCY	Nepalese rupee

A Buddhist temple near Kathmandu, capital of Nepal. It is festooned with colourful prayer flags.

NETHERLANDS

AREA	37,330 sq km
POPULATION	15,532,000
CAPITAL	Amsterdam
LANGUAGE	Dutch
RELIGION	Roman Catholic, Protestant
CURRENCY	Guilder

New Zealand

AREA	268,680 sq km
POPULATION	3,425,000
CAPITAL	Wellington
LANGUAGE	English, Maori
RELIGION	Christian
CURRENCY	New Zealand dollar

Geysers and hot springs near Rotorua on New Zealand's North Island. The government promote this volcanic area as a health resort.

Nicaragua

AREA	129,494 sq km
POPULATION	4,316,000
CAPITAL	Managua
LANGUAGE	Spanish
RELIGION	Roman Catholic
CURRENCY	Córdoba ora

NIGER

AREA	1,267,000 sq km
POPULATION	9,595,000
CAPITAL	Niamey
LANGUAGE	French, Hausa, Djerma
RELIGION	Muslim
CURRENCY	CFA franc

NIGERIA

AREA	923,770 sq km
POPULATION	104,430,000
CAPITAL	Abuja
LANGUAGE	English, Hausa, Yoruba, others
RELIGION	Muslim, Christian
CURRENCY	Naira

NORWAY

AREA	324,220 sq km
POPULATION	4,346,000
CAPITAL	Oslo
LANGUAGE	Norwegian
RELIGION	Lutheran
CURRENCY	Norwegian krone

OMAN

AREA	212,460 sq km
POPULATION	2,204,000
CAPITAL	Muscat
LANGUAGE	Arabic, English
RELIGION	Muslim
CURRENCY	Omani riyal

PAKISTAN

AREA	803,940 sq km
POPULATION	133,276,000
CAPITAL	Islamabad
LANGUAGE	Urdu, English, Punjabi
RELIGION	Muslim
CURRENCY	Pakistan rupee

The Shalimar Garden in Lahore, Pakistan. It was built in 1637 during the reign of Shah Jahan, one of the great Mughal emperors.

PANAMA

AREA	78,260 sq km
POPULATION	2,732,000
CAPITAL	Panama City
LANGUAGE	Spanish, English
RELIGION	Roman Catholic, Protestant
CURRENCY	Balboa

PAPUA NEW GUINEA

AREA	461,890 sq km
POPULATION	4,394,000
CAPITAL	Port Moresby
LANGUAGE	715 indigenous languages
RELIGION	Indigenous beliefs, Christian
CURRENCY	Kina

PARAGUAY

AREA	406,750 sq km
POPULATION	5,503,000
CAPITAL	Asunción
LANGUAGE	Spanish, Guaraní
RELIGION	Roman Catholic
CURRENCY	Guaraní

PERU

AREA	1,285,220 sq km
POPULATION	28,592,000
CAPITAL	Lima
LANGUAGE	Spanish, Quechua
RELIGION	Roman Catholic
CURRENCY	Sol

An aerial view of the remains of an Inca town discovered in Peru in 1911. The mountain of Machu Picchu rises in the background.

PHILIPPINES

AREA	300,000 sq km
POPULATION	74,900,000
CAPITAL	Manila
LANGUAGE	Pilipino, English
RELIGION	Roman Catholic, Muslim
CURRENCY	Philippine peso

POLAND

AREA	312,680 sq km
POPULATION	38,932,000
CAPITAL	Warsaw
LANGUAGE	Polish
RELIGION	Roman Catholic
CURRENCY	Zloty

PORTUGAL

AREA	92,080 sq km
POPULATION	10,600,000
CAPITAL	Lisbon
LANGUAGE	Portuguese
RELIGION	Roman Catholic
CURRENCY	Escudo

QATAR

AREA	11,000 sq km
POPULATION	549,000
CAPITAL	Doha
LANGUAGE	Arabic
RELIGION	Muslim
CURRENCY	Qatar riyal

ROMANIA

AREA	237,500 sq km
POPULATION	23,219,000
CAPITAL	Bucharest
LANGUAGE	Romanian, Hungarian, German
RELIGION	Orthodox
CURRENCY	Leu

RUSSIA

AREA	17,075,200 sq km
POPULATION	150,209,000
CAPITAL	Moscow
LANGUAGE	Russian, Slavic
RELIGION	Orthodox, Muslim
CURRENCY	Ruble

The towers of St Basil's Cathedral, built between 1554 and 1560 by Ivan the Terrible. It is one of Moscow's best-known sights.

RWANDA

AREA	26,340 sq km
POPULATION	8,290,000
CAPITAL	Kigali
LANGUAGE	Kinyarwanda, French
RELIGION	Indigenous beliefs, Roman Catholic
CURRENCY	Rwandese franc

SAINT KITTS AND NEVIS

AREA	269 sq km
POPULATION	41,300
CAPITAL	Basseterre
LANGUAGE	English
RELIGION	Protestant
CURRENCY	E. Caribbean dollar

SAINT LUCIA

AREA	620 sq km
POPULATION	157,800
CAPITAL	Castries
LANGUAGE	English, French patois
RELIGION	Roman Catholic
CURRENCY	E. Caribbean dollar

SAINT VINCENT AND THE GRENADINES

AREA	340 sq km
POPULATION	118,000
CAPITAL	Kingstown
LANGUAGE	English, French patois
RELIGION	Protestant, Roman Catholic
CURRENCY	E. Caribbean dollar

SAN MARINO

AREA	60 sq km
POPULATION	24,200
CAPITAL	San Marino
LANGUAGE	Italian
RELIGION	Roman Catholic
CURRENCY	Italian lira

SÃO TOMÉ AND PRINCIPE

AREA	960 sq km
POPULATION	144,000
CAPITAL	São Tomé
LANGUAGE	Portuguese
RELIGION	Roman Catholic, Protestant
CURRENCY	Dobra

SAUDI ARABIA

AREA	1,960,582 sq km
POPULATION	19,418,000
CAPITAL	Riyadh
LANGUAGE	Arabic
RELIGION	Muslim
CURRENCY	Saudi Arabian riyal

A group of Saudi Arabian men and boys take part in an exuberant folk dance.

SENEGAL

AREA	196,190 sq km
POPULATION	9,280,000
CAPITAL	Dakar
LANGUAGE	French, Wolof, Pulaar
RELIGION	Muslim
CURRENCY	CFA franc

SERBIA AND MONTENEGRO

AREA	102,350 sq km
POPULATION	11,158,000
CAPITAL	Belgrade
LANGUAGE	Serbo-Croat
RELIGION	Orthodox, Muslim
CURRENCY	Dinar

SEYCHELLES

AREA	455 sq km
POPULATION	78,600
CAPITAL	Victoria
LANGUAGE	English, French, Creole
RELIGION	Roman Catholic
CURRENCY	Seychelles rupee

SIERRA LEONE

AREA	71,740 sq km
POPULATION	4,878,000
CAPITAL	Freetown
LANGUAGE	English, Mende, Temne
RELIGION	Muslim, indigenous beliefs
CURRENCY	Leone

SINGAPORE

AREA	632.6 sq km
POPULATION	2,920,000
CAPITAL	Singapore
LANGUAGE	Chinese, Malay, Tamil, English
RELIGION	Buddhist, Muslim, Christian, others
CURRENCY	Singapore dollar

Marina Bay and the business district of Singapore. This is the largest port in South-east Asia and a major world trading centre.

SLOVAK REPUBLIC

AREA	48,845 sq km
POPULATION	5,461,000
CAPITAL	Bratislava
LANGUAGE	Slovak
RELIGION	Roman Catholic, Atheist, Protestant
CURRENCY	Koruna

SLOVENIA

AREA	20,296 sq km
POPULATION	2,057,000
CAPITAL	Ljubljana
LANGUAGE	Slovenian, Serbo-Croat
RELIGION	Roman Catholic
CURRENCY	Dinar

SOLOMON ISLANDS

AREA	28,450 sq km
POPULATION	412,000
CAPITAL	Honiara
LANGUAGE	Melanesian pidgin
RELIGION	Protestant
CURRENCY	Solomon Island dollar

SOMALIA

AREA	637,657 sq km
POPULATION	8,492,000
CAPITAL	Mogadishu
LANGUAGE	Somali, Arabic
RELIGION	Islam
CURRENCY	Somali shilling

SOUTH AFRICA

AREA	1,219,912 sq km
POPULATION	46,272,000
CAPITAL	Pretoria
LANGUAGE	Afrikaans, English
RELIGION	Roman Catholic, Protestant
CURRENCY	South African rand

The waterfront area of Cape Town, South Africa. Cape Town is a major port and industrial city. The settlement was founded in 1652.

SPAIN

AREA	504,750 sq km
POPULATION	39,510,000
CAPITAL	Madrid
LANGUAGE	Spanish
RELIGION	Roman Catholic
CURRENCY	Peseta

SRI LANKA

AREA	65,610 sq km
POPULATION	18,554,000
CAPITAL	Colombo
LANGUAGE	Sinhala, Tamil
RELIGION	Buddhist, Hindu
CURRENCY	Sri Lankan rupee

A fine example of a Buddhist stupa, a dome-shaped monument for housing relics, at Polonnaruva, Sri Lanka.

SUDAN

AREA	2,505,810 sq km
POPULATION	30,827,000
CAPITAL	Khartoum
LANGUAGE	Arabic, Nubian, Ta Bedawie, others
RELIGION	Sunni Muslim, indigenous beliefs
CURRENCY	Sudanese pound

SURINAM

AREA	163,270 sq km
POPULATION	436,000
CAPITAL	Paramaribo
LANGUAGE	Dutch, English, Sranang, Tongo
RELIGION	Protestant, Hindu, Muslim
CURRENCY	Surinam guilder

SWAZILAND

AREA	17,360 sq km
POPULATION	998,000
CAPITAL	Mbabane
LANGUAGE	siSwati, English
RELIGION	Christian, indigenous beliefs
CURRENCY	Lilangeni

SWEDEN

AREA	449,964 sq km
POPULATION	8,862,000
CAPITAL	Stockholm
LANGUAGE	Swedish
RELIGION	Lutheran
CURRENCY	Swedish krona

SWITZERLAND

AREA	41,290 sq km
POPULATION	7,125,000
CAPITAL	Bern
LANGUAGE	German, French
RELIGION	Protestant, Roman Catholic
CURRENCY	Swiss franc

The Swiss Alps near the peak of the Jungfrau (4158 metres/13,632 feet). A railway climbs 3454 metres (11,333 feet) up the mountain pass.

SYRIA

AREA	185,180 sq km
POPULATION	16,025,000
CAPITAL	Damascus
LANGUAGE	Arabic, others
RELIGION	Muslim, Christian
CURRENCY	Syrian pound

TAIWAN

AREA	35,890 sq km
POPULATION	21,700,000
CAPITAL	Taipei
LANGUAGE	Mandarin Chinese
RELIGION	Buddhist, Confucist, Taoist
CURRENCY	New Taiwan dollar

TAJIKISTAN

AREA	143,100 sq km
POPULATION	6,315,000
CAPITAL	Dushanbe
LANGUAGE	Tajic
RELIGION	Sunni Muslim
CURRENCY	Ruble

TANZANIA

AREA	945,090 sq km
POPULATION	29,432,000
CAPITAL	Dodoma
LANGUAGE	Swahili, English
RELIGION	Christian, Muslim
CURRENCY	Tanzanian shilling

THAILAND

AREA	514,000 sq km
POPULATION	61,018,000
CAPITAL	Bangkok
LANGUAGE	Thai
RELIGION	Buddhist
CURRENCY	Baht

TOGO

AREA	56,790 sq km
POPULATION	4,568,000
CAPITAL	Lomé
LANGUAGE	French, Ewe, Mina, Dagomba
RELIGION	Indigenous beliefs, Christian, Muslim
CURRENCY	CFA franc

TONGA

AREA	748 sq km
POPULATION	106,000
CAPITAL	Nuku'alofa
LANGUAGE	English, Tongan
RELIGION	Christian
CURRENCY	Pa'anga

TRINIDAD AND TOBAGO

AREA	5,130 sq km
POPULATION	1,272,000
CAPITAL	Port-of-Spain
LANGUAGE	English, Spanish, Hindi, French
RELIGION	Christian, Hindu
CURRENCY	Trinidad and Tobago dollar

A colourful carnival procession in Trinidad.

TUNISIA

AREA	163,610 sq km
POPULATION	9,030,000
CAPITAL	Tunis
LANGUAGE	Arabic, French
RELIGION	Muslim
CURRENCY	Tunisian dinar

TURKEY

AREA	780,560 sq km
POPULATION	64,654,000
CAPITAL	Ankara
LANGUAGE	Turkish
RELIGION	Muslim
CURRENCY	Turkish lira

The Ayasofya Mosque, Istanbul, Turkey. Istanbul is an ancient city which began life as Byzantium in Roman times.

TURKMENISTAN

AREA	488,100 sq km
POPULATION	4,155,000
CAPITAL	Ashkhabad
LANGUAGE	Turkmen, Russian
RELIGION	Muslim, Orthodox
CURRENCY	Ruble

TUVALU

AREA	26 sq km
POPULATION	10,100
CAPITAL	Funafuti
LANGUAGE	Tuvaluan, English
RELIGION	Protestant
CURRENCY	Australian dollar

UGANDA

AREA	236,040 sq km
POPULATION	20,013,000
CAPITAL	Kampala
LANGUAGE	English, Tribal
RELIGION	Roman Catholic, Protestant, Muslim
CURRENCY	Uganda shilling

UKRAINE

AREA	603,700 sq km
POPULATION	51,888,000
CAPITAL	Kiev
LANGUAGE	Ukrainian, Russian
RELIGION	Orthodox
CURRENCY	Ruble

UNITED ARAB EMIRATES

AREA 75,881 sq km
POPULATION 4,103,000
CAPITAL Abu Dhabi
LANGUAGE Arabic, English, Persian
RELIGION Muslim
CURRENCY UAE dirham

UNITED KINGDOM

AREA 244,820 sq km
POPULATION 58,452,000
CAPITAL London
LANGUAGE English
RELIGION Protestant, Roman Catholic
CURRENCY British pound

The Houses of Parliament on the River Thames, London. It contains the House of Commons and the House of Lords.

UNITED STATES OF AMERICA

AREA	9,372,610 sq km
POPULATION	266,504,000
CAPITAL	Washington, D.C
LANGUAGE	English, Spanish
RELIGION	Protestant, Roman Catholic
CURRENCY	U.S. dollar

URUGUAY

AREA	176,220 sq km
POPULATION	3,247,000
CAPITAL	Montevideo
LANGUAGE	Spanish
RELIGION	Roman Catholic
CURRENCY	Uruguayan peso

UZBEKISTAN

AREA	447,400 sq km
POPULATION	23,578,000
CAPITAL	Tashkent
LANGUAGE	Uzbek, Russian
RELIGION	Muslim, Orthodox
CURRENCY	Ruble

VANUATU

AREA	14,760 sq km
POPULATION	178,000
CAPITAL	Port-Vila
LANGUAGE	Bislama, English, French
RELIGION	Christian
CURRENCY	Vatu

VATICAN CITY

AREA	0.44 sq km
POPULATION	830
CAPITAL	Vatican City
LANGUAGE	Italian, Latin
RELIGION	Roman Catholic
CURRENCY	Vatican lira

A view of St Peter's, the largest church in the world, in the Vatican City, seat of government of the Roman Catholic Church.

VENEZUELA

AREA	912,050 sq km
POPULATION	21,446,000
CAPITAL	Caracas
LANGUAGE	Spanish
RELIGION	Roman Catholic
CURRENCY	Bolívar

VIETNAM

AREA	329,560 sq km
POPULATION	75,665,000
CAPITAL	Hanoi
LANGUAGE	Vietnamese
RELIGION	Buddhist, Taoist, Christian
CURRENCY	Dong

WESTERN SAHARA

AREA	266,000 sq km
POPULATION	222,000
CAPITAL	El Aaiún
LANGUAGE	Arabic
RELIGION	Muslim
CURRENCY	CFA franc

WESTERN SAMOA

AREA	2,860 sq km
POPULATION	214,000
CAPITAL	Apia
LANGUAGE	Samoan, English,
RELIGION	Protestant, Roman Catholic
CURRENCY	Tala

YEMEN

AREA	527,790 sq km
POPULATION	15,320,000
CAPITAL	San'a
LANGUAGE	Arabic
RELIGION	Muslim
CURRENCY	Yemen riyal

ZAÏRE

AREA	2,345,410 sq km
POPULATION	45,461,000
CAPITAL	Kinshasa
LANGUAGE	French, Tribal
RELIGION	Christian, Kimbanguist
CURRENCY	Zaïre

ZAMBIA

AREA	752,610 sq km
POPULATION	9,700,000
CAPITAL	Lusaka
LANGUAGE	English, Tribal
RELIGION	Christian, Muslim
CURRENCY	Zambian kwacha

ZIMBABWE

AREA	390,580 sq km
POPULATION	11,338,000
CAPITAL	Harare
LANGUAGE	English, Shona, Sindebele
RELIGION	Christian, indigenous beliefs
CURRENCY	Zimbabwe dollar

Victoria Falls on the border between Zimbabwe and Zambia drops 128 metres (420 feet) over a 1.6-km (1-mile) wide rock ledge.

GLOSSARY

Badge: An emblem or other device displayed on a flag.

Banner: A rectangular flag used by a king, prince, duke, or other noble. The coat of arms of the owner covered the banner's entire surface.

Canton: The four quarters of a flag are called cantons, especially the upper quarter of the hoist, the upper left hand corner of the flag The canton is some-times also called the union.

Colours: The national and regimental or armorial flags that are carried into combat by infantry regiments. The term also applies to the national ensign that is flown aboard a navy ship.

Ensign: A special flag that is based on a country's national flag but which is kept for exclusive use onboard naval ships or merchant ships. Great Britain has a white ensign that is flown from naval ships, a red ensign for merchant ships and a blue ensign for merchant ships that are commanded by an officer in the Naval Reserve. The United States flag, on the other hand, serves as a national flag, a naval ensign and also as a civil ensign.

Field: The background colour of each division of a flag.

Fly: The edge of a flag farthest from the staff.

Halyard: The rope by which a flag is raised on a flagpole.

Hoist: The edge of a flag nearest the staff. Also, used as a verb, means to raise a flag.

Hoist rope: The rope from which a flag is flown on a flagpole.

Jack: A flag flown at the bow of warships when they are at anchor. Great Britain's Union Jack combines the crosses of St George, St Andrew, and St David on a blue field. The USA's Union Jack carries 50 white stars on a blue field.

Staff: A small pole from which a flag is flown.

Standard: A flag that is coloured according to the owner's livery and displays the owner's badge or badges instead of his arms. The term 'national standard' is used to describe the national and regimental flags carried by mounted or motorized regiments.

Union: A flag or device on a flag that symbolises the union of countries or states.

WORLD FACTS

Total surface area: 510,072,000 sq km

Land area: 148,940,000 sq km
(29.2% of the world is land)

Water area: 361,132,000 sq km
(70.8% of the world is water)

Coastline: 356,000 km

Highest point: Mount Everest 8,848 metres

Lowest point: Dead Sea, 392 metres below sea level

Deepest part of the ocean: Marianas Trench, 10,924 metres

WORLD LAND USE

Arable land: 10%

Permanent crops: 1%

Meadows and pasture: 24%

Forest and woodland: 31%

Other: 34%

POPULATION FACTS

World population: 5,733,687,096 (estimated figure for July 1995)

Population growth rate: 1.5% per annum (1995 estimate)

Birth rate: 24 births per 1000 population (1995 estimate)

Death rate: 9 deaths per 1000 population (1995 estimate)

Average life expectancy: males, 61 years; females, 64 years

THE WORLD ECONOMY

Gross World Product: $30.7 trillion (1994 estimate)

Average global rate of inflation (all countries): 25%

Average unemployment rate: 30%